LOVE
POEMS

by

Nathan Delfim

AFTER LOVE AND FEAR, THERE'S PRIDE

There is pride after love, fear and tears; there is night following the rain.

The chair that only has one light.

The dream that you'll come back safe after memories; another day, after sleep

I am waiting to live.

The happiness of thinking about your love after moments of despair

No thought could move a stone.

Hunger and pain are the only things left after all sacrifice.

Losses and gains: The promises and passions

You are my only love, which waits on the wind

You must now defend yourself.

AFTER YOU LEAVE,

I will become a tree

If you go, I'll become a lonely tree, sitting on the hillside and loving the wind and sunshine, waiting for you to come back to me, even if it takes centuries.

My tall branches will provide shade for birds, and bright-eyed creatures. When I am satisfied with my progress, I will spread out the branches of my leaves like wings.

But oh! The moment is every minute

You'll be missed with all the passion in the world, as I gaze endlessly at the road.

You must not be there to empty the wind.

DO NOT LOVE ME YET

You must not fall in love with me, as I am still only a thin moon. A scimitar around the heart

Touching too quickly or with too much force is dangerous.

It is important that I grow more full of golden light before I am touched.

You need to rule the night and smile at my world.

What roads and fields are in my territory?

I will dull the ecstasy of my newfound jubilation with sophomoric pain.

The love I seek is from a blank, dark boy.

We might fear and groan in our ignorance.

Then, I will be a bowl of silver and I will know exactly what I am capable of holding.

We could also try to love

You are still young enough to enjoy life.

DO YOU WANT ME? WHAT'S THE MATTER?

What's the matter? What is the problem? What's the matter? Want the smell of roses without the actual rose? You want the moans without the chatter of love?

Do you think that our love could be like a tomb? Is this the only way out of my suffering?

Give your fantasy some space?

She's amazing, but after a few months?

I might get bored? What about something more interesting? Filling in a sweater to make it tighter.

Might flash me a quick come-on smile?

Don't you want to commit yourself yet? To one future and one kiss only? Think about what you could miss, and wait for a more lucrative bet.

Well, fine! Why do you follow me around like a jackal all day and night?

When my interests seem to shift, are you sure what you want, then?

You go crazy when you hear me laugh at a guy's jokes. It is nasty and bordering on sadistic.

What if someone touched my stuff?

Draw a line between what I and you can do. Take away your fear and let go of it.

It takes two to smother.

It is impossible to love freedom and be a lover at the same time, unless you are a fool.

DREAMS DO COME TRUE

When they overcome their despair and stumbling into the everyday, dreams do become real.

The transformation is beyond repair

If it could pass as something real, we would not sail to paradise if its shoals were hidden.

It is also with love that I say: The dream, long longed-for, and now attained, Can no longer be considered a fantasy, but an emperor undressed.

It must be shocking to see us naked in our unaccustomed shame.

We must love and embrace it.

We must accept love for what it is, so that dreams can still be realized.

Make our life anew.

EACH TRUTH IS A SCRIM ACROSS THE DARKNESS

Every truth is a thin scrim over the darkness. Most of what we would like to see is not visible.

In pale moonlight, we drive along sheer cliffs. Uncertain of our location or destination.

If we let our head make the decisions, we lose out because we can't see.

If we let our desires take over, we lose out because we are unable to achieve what we desire.

As we inch our way along dreamy rocky ridges, we know that always and forever must be lost.

Darkness will never end.

It is less important which route we take.

It is important to be who we are; the gifts that we already have, and those which we will develop; the ecstasy in loving completely.

We are greater than our minds could ever comprehend.

Know that the love you have for someone will end with pain. Pay the price for being a fool.

Never lose your passion for life.

EVEN THOUGH WE FIGHT A LOT, I LOVE YOU

Even though I hate you, even when we argue a lot.

The stakes are very high, we fight I believe. Sometimes I am so angry I can't stand you. But beneath my anger, I would cry.

You are my only guide and destiny. I am driven by an insatiable need to be in control of you.

My poor love is entangled with my pride. I'm aware that it's not fair for me to attempt to shape you. Ah, love! Love me in spite of my anger, which rises as a wave beneath the moon. My only judge and jury is:

Change is not coming soon, I know. Love has a hard time letting the beloved go

A person that is so deeply loved.

EVERYTHING I HAVE DONE, I AM

All I have done is for you.

All I Am, I Am

You will be moved by the hope that your heart moves.

While you are away I love you.

You'll be loved as if our love would last until you turn grey.

My love, we will be together until the day that both of us are gray.

You're my home, and I will love you as much as I do right now.

THE FATE IS OFTEN THE FULCRUM OF PASSION

The passion of the flow of the fate is often a filament that illuminates the world.

May fortunes be a sway for love and not just chance.

Love is the constant tide that keeps the years flowing.

Love is the best expression of fate.

It is impossible to find a better confession.

GIFTS ARE NOT ALWAYS FREE

The best gifts aren't always free.

The giver is curious: Do you like my gift? Even burdens can bring intense joy.

Recently, I was unable to differentiate between gifts and burdens.

Indian elephants hauled seventeen tons of logs made from teak over the Himalayas.

We all have our own versions of the mistake.

The gift of love is an amazing thing.

The rattling of their demands is a sign that burdens are hiding. We all want to know if we are a burden, or a blessing.

Few people understand that in order to give a true gift, one must also receive.

While burdens are dressed up in bows and ribbons.

The guilt of refusing a present is regret. Mirrors can be used to address any lingering doubts.

The elephants were happy and sweaty yesterday. They also seemed to have gained a lot of wisdom.

HE ONLY CARES THAT I AM HAPPY

He only cares that I am happy.

I've was not with me.

Some seek the love's wind traces.

Some search for the love inside. All my pleasures are in his possession, or does he only desire joy?

All claim his compassion

No Dark Soul is all on its own.

Giving so, naturally.

Each day, he ignites the love within me.

Like candles lit by the sun on a stone.

HOLD ME TO YOUR WILLING HEART

Help me weep and hold me close to you willing heart.

I need it so that I can fall apart.

Allow the truth to cut into me, so that I may finally bleed. And cleanse myself of pain I will not now admit.

Because I've found myself to light, I can live with joy.

I will not let the love that bonds me to you be destroyed by night.

Yet I am certain that I will gain the peace I seek.

My love must be washed away by the pain.

HOW CAN I FIGHT WITH MY BEST FRIEND?

What if I fight my best friend with him? The landscape has been destroyed by the wind.

Black lava where once there were gardens and fields. Black lava where once there were flowers and fields.

The blackness is broken by the appearance of some grass shoots. Slowly, love returns.

We go on for days in whispers. He calls and I cry.

Ah! Now I am afraid of the mountain. I walk around it trembling and ready for its blow.

The beauty of life is also its pain.

Now that I am aware, I can love.

HOW CAN I BE SO SURE THAT I WILL LOVE YOU?

What makes me so sure that I will love you no matter what happens in the future?

The time is like the cave where our torches only show us our mind's circumference.

Love is more about will than passion. Passion may initially sustain will. Love is chosen the same way as faith, because that's the way heaven looks.

I love you more than an ocean. You are richer in beauty than coral seas.

It is a precious gift that I will not give up.

HOW DID I LOSE MY BABY BLUE EYES?

What happened to your blue baby eyes and the smile which lit my skies? Was it that I said to you? What did I say that sent you away?

We can sometimes find ourselves alone and lost when we try to go with the flow.

How did you miss the turn after a kiss that told me I was wrong?

What made you leave my heart so quickly without my being aware?

What have you seen deep within me that I didn't know existed?

In the dark, we drive down empty and strange roads. We are suddenly thrown into pain.

After we lose we realize that we have done the same thing again.

HOW OFTEN ARE THINGS SIMPLE AND RIGHT?

When is it that everything just makes
sense? Every day, we face moments of despair.

There is love in even the darkest of
hours. Nobody can explain why our flower
opens to the sunlight when one among all of the
others.

We could in truth love anyone. But choosing
does not require a test. How many times does
an angel change our identity by touching us?

Love is a bright star lit by the holy flames that
burn deep inside.

I AM AFRAID TO LOVE, BUT I STILL LOVE YOU

I'm afraid of loving you, but I do. It's like I can walk through a wall.

I can't be stopped by the wall. You still need me, but I also need the wall.

Someday, I'm sure we will find ourselves in a beautiful field Surrounded with the blessings of the skies.

Wanting you, without knowing why I need you.

You might reject my need. Your laughter and tears make me completely myself. You are the flower and I am the thin reed.

YOU ARE OF THE CULTIVATION, I AM FROM THE DESERT

You are a cultivator, I'm a desert: To me simplicity is desolation, and to me it is simple.

You seek elegance, quiet, and restoration, while I look for heat, thirst, or agony. You are the beach, I'm the ocean:

It's not that you want less waves; it's more than I can produce. You prefer tranquil bays; I like the roar of rollers. In me is a wild emptiness; in yours is a calm core. You are like the lake, I'm like a stream: I scream over rocks, and you make reflections.

As I hurl myself forward, bones and branches are breaking.

Then you absorb the wake.

It may seem obvious that extremes like these should never be mixed;

Love can bring even the most contradictory things together.

I DIDN'T GET A CHANCE TO SAY I LOVE YOU

You were gone before we got that far. Before we reached that point, you were already gone. Now I need you more than ever.

When I search for you you're not there.

How can I know without your presence that you will never forget me?

What a void! What I am feeling is a cold, thin, airy, and void.

When I am alone, sometimes, when you are holding me close, my desire for you is a constant pain.

I am surrounded by a jumble of memories. It's impossible to think that I will never see you again.

I DON'T KNOW HOW WE GET INTO THESE FIGHTS

How do we end up in these fights?

After them, I looked back on the ashes

I am more shocked than injured, such as in the case of a crash of a small plane.

Illing numb by strange and unearthly light. **Oh**h! How I would love to get off this plane **R**ushing its rendezvous in tears!

Age is just a mask to hide my timid fears.

Yet I would die before I caused you pain.

MY HEART FEELS LIKE IT IS BLEEDING

It feels like my heart is bleeding on a counter.

It is as if a flood of pain has erupted.

The pain is all that I can do.

It is impossible for me to imagine a life without you.

Ah, God! Oh, God!

I want to hold you again, no matter what.

I want to hold you again and tell you my love.

If you do not feel like moving, then return to the dust.

YOU ARE THE ONE I LOVE AND THAT IS WHERE I FIND MY HAPPINESS

Love you makes me happy.

Even if my love has not been returned, I am willing to wait. In the woods, I can pray.

The beauty and grace of my innermost being.

The unity of love that must be desired is not there yet, even though you hold me close and we kiss.

It's not what I want; it's how you want me. This is the truth.

The only thing I want is to be free.

The moon's patience is lonely, and it will not last forever.

YOU HAVE A MONSTER CRUSH ON YOU

Super-dinosaurs, I'm in love with you!

The pain is so intense that it reaches my chest and throat. I still beg to have more.

If you are away, I will miss you. My heart will be full of sand.

But when I'm here, my stupid fear won't allow me to touch your hand.

You have me so wrapped around you that I can't sleep or eat.

I drift away from the words and let my thoughts fade.

It's not my fault that you have a crush on me.

Please rescue me if possible.

You can hold my hands and tell me you love me. God! What a good thing!

YOU MUST HAVE BEEN IN PAIN BECAUSE I KNOW I HURT YOU

You must be in pain. I am sure I have caused it. Further, I am aware that I've lost your confidence.

If I could go back in time, I would relive that exact moment to rewrite my recklessness and passion.

We sometimes have to give up what we love most in order to understand our needs.

Playing with our lives until they are almost gone

Dare to be in the dark, even though we are bleeding. You are as important to me as a rose must be in the sun.

Turn its empty radiance into glory

As a country needs to know the secrets of its forgotten history.

You may now trust me even more because of my transgression.

YOU LOOK AT ME AND I THINK: "I CANNOT LIVE."

You are the one I dream about. It's true; I do know that I can. But I have to give.

It is my heart's room to say it how it appears. Romance needs a language that fits the feelings.

There can be no ceiling or floor for love:

I love you too much to let it go. When I tell you that I can't live without your love, I mean it.

You can imagine the pain I'm in;

When I say that I always dream of you, the moon will be happy again.

It is the sun that reveals to all cold, hard truths. But it's my duty to light up love through poetry.

YOU ARE AS LOVED BY A VALLEY AS I AM

As a river flows through a valley, or as an inscription on a sheet of paper the music it produces.

You are as important to me as the moon is to the sun.

As if a soul on the search for faith is saved by a sign.

Meadows and you are both a part me.

As a heart is a song, renewing its value.

You are my love as much as a bird loves the air or a seafarer loves the ocean.

As a powerful wave searches for sand. But, ah! Do you love me?

I LOVE YOU EVEN THOUGH I KNOW

Even though you don't show me any love, I still love you.

You are the icy springs of my hidden ecstasy.

You are my all-night companion. I sleep with you.

Your face is all I can think about.

The sea is black, and I am alone.

Only you can calm down my Galilee, dear one.

YOU ARE THE ONLY ONE I LOVE WITH ALL MY HEART

You are the only person I will ever love.

Your earth, sky and sea are mine, as well as my sun, moon and stars.

I love you so much that my feelings for you go below both the life and death.

When I have drawn my final faint breath, it will be so deep that the void must still remain.

Time will disappear if you hold me for many months or years.

Your lips will become my lips; your face my face, and your tears my tears.

We will become one odd person - all intertwined in bliss.

No matter if you are a man, woman or dead person, all that matters is a simple kiss.

WHAT I MUST ACCEPT BUT CANNOT BE

What I cannot accept, but must accept. When I look at you, my heart breaks.

Although you may not be dead to others, I consider that you have died.

It's still a mystery what happened to love.

In vain, I search through the emptiness of our past. What cannot be, I accept.

It is now clear that someone shares the same offhand phrase as you. Your tender tongue feels drained. . . Although you're not dead yourself, I consider you to be dead.

You cannot ignore my pain:

The same tune I repeat.

What I cannot accept, but must accept.

But I also know that this is just my way to hold you once again.

Although you may not be dead to others, I consider that you have died.

But I still cannot bring myself to let you go.

Our love might be left behind in some form. What cannot be, I accept.

Although you may not be dead, I consider that you are.

I USED BECOME COMPLETELY CRUEL AND HEARTLESS

I was completely heartless and cruel, using girls then throwing them away.

When I was a child, my hunger used to be angry and bitter.

No idea why nor much looking inside.

I thought that the purpose of my life was to enjoy myself, in whatever form it might be. The feelings of a woman were her own.

It was never a good idea to sacrifice yourself.

With just a slight twinge of guilt, I went in search of my lonely ecstasy.

Even when I was looking for a friend, I only cared about myself.

Like God, we create our worlds in our image. Mine was a stone metropolis

All souls are either fools or Cynics. Doomed only to enjoy themselves.

Then I was in love with you, and your happiness seemed to mean more than mine. My heart started to glow like the sun as flowers and greenery grew in the desert.

Like a breeze, I moved across the sea, and like a star, I burst into darkness.

Like a song, I held the love of my life in my hand. And just like an angel, I knew this was what had to be done.

The lies I told to justify my greed have proven me wrong.

Love is to feel the joy of living.

If I loved as much, then I would be loved.

I could let someone know about me, without feeling shame.

If I knew that I would be able to retrieve my own self, then it was possible for me to give myself.

You can know me for all I am.

If you don't love me, then so be it. But I understand.

YOU MAKE ME SMILE AS I WANT TO SEE YOU DO

You make me smile, and I'd like to do the same for you.

You ask me what I'm thinking. What am I thinking? You can't know what I think.

The stars are you, the sky is empty.

There is an ever-flowing yearning in me

It is a need to bring an end which will never come. You are the only person who can make me feel like myself.

No wisdom has ever delved into this truth.

This is the angel I so desperately want to be.

My life has the beauty of a passionate love

You can see the wind blowing through a person.

YOU CAN MAKE YOUR HEART BEAT JUST FOR ME

Want to beat your heart just for you? I need a real love to fill my life of loneliness.

I have dated many guys, and looked for a very long time.

No one I was walking with kept pace with me.

The best friends walk well together. We seem to fit together, like we were cut from the same cloth.

To go together, zigzags complementary.

Now I'm more than just a friend.

It's not the first time I mention my love. You don't know what's going on in my heart. If you could catch a falling, burning star I would be happy to make you feel loved.

WISH I COULD BE WITH YOU

You are my favorite person. I love you.

If I had your worries, I would take them away.

When you smile, your joy will light up the drawers.

You can feel the joy in my heart.

All the rain can turn into a rainbow at the Sun.

All our loneliness could fade away like mist into the sky.

Remembering the hard, sad times that happened in the past.

You cannot be here and I can't come back right away.

Our dreams are the places where we play and laugh.

The life we desire will come to pass;

Love can transform the most harsh light into gold.

THIS POEM WOULD BE BETTER IF IT WERE A PIXIE DUST

This poem is like pixie Dust that you can throw in your eyes

You will see that there is beauty beneath my sad mask.

You would be in my arms. I'd weave you a magical spell

This is what I would say to make you fall in love with me at any time.

My simple words are like rain in summer

It is as if the drums that beat on fields, hills and in hearts suddenly vanish.

Even though I might be able to make you blossom, your fragile grace is what turns the world around.

Gaze in agonizing loneliness at someone else's Face.

The long chain of unbroken links is what we crave.

Loved ones who are unloved and lovers who do not love.

The sun is essential to trees.

It is impossible to avoid falling in love with someone who loves another.

THE WAY I SAY I LOVE YOU IS WRONG

Sorry for how I said I loved you.

This kind of conversation is way too early. It is impossible for me to stop loving you.

This truth is its own death sentence. When a lie betrays itself I ask myself: could it be that this truth is true?

Could my sweet obsession with you be a result of ignorance?

What I really feel is the only thing I can know. It lies below all reason or law.

It may just be that I am a fool, but my love for you will always remain deep, rich and true.

The truth will come out in the end, if we do not.

You will not be my lover for long.

IN THE DAYLIGHT, YOU'RE A HAUNTING MELODY

More beautiful than the scene before my eyes. In sunlight you are a haunting melodies. In darkness you become my symphony,

I don't know any other connections.

So Are You Nestled With Me Night and Day?

Your Missing Self Transmuted Into Song, Or Walking Closely Next To Me On My Way,

Unleashing All the Love I Long For.

IN MOURNING, SEA FOG

Seafog makes small details visible when in mourning. Pearls adhere to the petals.

The glass fringes the pine needles. Sea waves crash against the rocks.

It breaks when you heave back.

What is the beauty of a wild rose? What have you given me, do you know?

IT SOMETIMES SEEMS SO FOOLISH TO PERSIST

Sometimes it seems foolish to continue when years and miles separate us. It's hard to resist the midnight love of despair

A darkness grips you, a void that is crushing. . . The thought of quitting is like dying:

I could feel the same pain. The alleyways of the hollow years. The python wrapped itself around my breath. My eyes cracked under the strain of tears.

Ah, my darling! Now we feel pain.

We are grateful for the love that fills our heart with light. We are sure that this joy will be shared again.

We can only hope that dreams will help us get through this night of anguish. We dip and glide as we soaring across the sea.

It's not just our lips that are apart; it's also the thoughts we have.

IT'S AMAZING HOW I FEEL WHEN I AM AROUND YOU

You make me feel so good.

My heart pound when you enter a room. When I see you, my first thought is: "My God!" What a beautiful thing!

Everything I am blooms.

You must be mine. Not just as a possession, but as an aim.

It's almost impossible to imagine:

Free devotion to another soul

It was as if I was about to go into heaven

You will be condemned to death within an hour.

I can't stop thinking about you. You are the only reason my mind is so agitated.

JUST AS THE ENTIRE WORLD HAS BEEN CONNECTED

As the world is now connected, we can all live together.

Our inner worlds are now intersecting:

Love can now call from anywhere in the world. The depth of our keyboard discussions has reached the sources of pain and joy.

One day, even though one now writes in the night, passion for writing will not be a barrier.

When lovers are reunited under the rain and sun.

LET ME LOVE YOU WELL, IF NOT TOO LONG

I will love you, but not for too long. Passion is the lover of air. Enjoying what is around, belonging to that which we all must belong. You will become a part of the sweet melody I sing, as I am of yours. We may part more fair, and enriched with what we have shared.

You will be more enthralled by the life you live, gentler and stronger. Passion is something one shouldn't waste:

Fear of losing the best part of life, losing our ecstasy, which we are meant to experience.

We must enjoy what is given us to be able to do.

What our love reveals.

MY LOVE, LOSE YOURSELF IN LUST

My love, let yourself be swept away by lust;
enjoy me like a thing.

Your soul is your slave; my flesh, your fantasia.

All your voices, please, let them sing!

Not a single ecstasy lost

What a sweet reward could a sin grant?

The secret place where dreams become wounds
festers for lack of attention, untended, but with
stealth.

Calliope tunes are inexhaustible for them,

Love's real wealth is found in trust.

LOVE COMES TO THE ONE WHO LOVES

When you love someone, and find your joy in their happiness, or tears in theirs, then it is easy to fall in love.

Gifts that are buoyant go to those in need

Through the wasted years of their lives. Power is not a virtue, but weakness.

No one has the power to force affection. Love may be passionate to those who are self-absorbed, but passion is looking for its own reflection. The tide of love is always changing.

The moon gives and receives as it goes.

The high cliffs are weathered, rough and eroded. Love becomes the cause for love.

Double knots are difficult to untie.

LOVE IS OBSTACLES ENOUGH FOR THEM, THEY SAY

They say that love is already a difficult thing. Why would they add the race as an obstacle?

Two backgrounds so diverse can't share one space. The harsh realities of the world can't be kept at bay by love.

Ah, love! Such trite advice should be rewarded! Life is full of challenges, but also grace.

Men and women live in the same tiny space. We should not fear that our love will betray.

The love of everyday life is a vein in the rock that runs through it like liquid fire. It makes ordinary moments shine.

As we age, may we cherish it?

Our drab clay is inspired by the breath of our breath. The touch transforms all that we are.

LOVE IS LIKE AN LARGE WHITES CAT

The love is like the large white cat sitting on its paws.

The dog is a creature that lives according to its own rules.

Whatever you may say, it will come and go as the wind decides.

You will find that the closer you get to it, the faster it disappears.

When you're satisfied, sit in the sunshine

You can be alone with your own thoughts and desires, without anyone else.

It comes out, almost as though in fear that you will forget.

The dog will jump up and purr in your lap.

LOVE IS NEVER EASY

The song of love is a beautiful way to turn life into a song.

Love can transform any circumstance.

No one can be tempted by anger or despair

The love of God cannot be converted to Grace and made whole.

The bliss of knowing that someone else finds pleasure in your happiness.

What a sweet gift to give to someone who has given to you.

Selflessness is giving more than oneself.

There is no joy in the world, with all its searing madness and dreary sorrow.

One truth is more beautiful than anyone could ever bear

When they turn, they will find each other.

LOVE LINGERS IN THE ALLEYWAYS

The smell of love wafts through the streets and lingers on the sidewalks.

You knock on my double door but never come inside.

The love of the world is found in all entrances and retreats.

Two doors away from the sin, he scurries and flies past faint applause.

Ah! Ah!

Because I am afraid of the heavy chains that jangle when my joy is rejoicing.

When I ask for more, it makes me fear that the floods will come.

Quiet, please. I'd rather gain from such tempests than to be disturbed.

LOVE ME IN THE CIRCLE OF YOUR EVENING

You can love me even in your sleepy morning dreams. Love me beneath ambitious plans

When they are slowing down, some seasoning can be used.

You do not have to worry about me, as long as you can come home. Both of us have miles to explore in paradise:

I will be there where you brave heart is retreating.

You will be loved in times of joy and sorrow, hope and laughter.

We can share all those days when our thoughts are haunted, and we can also feel the ever-present undertow.

LOVE REDEEMS THE PASSIONS OF THE MOMENT

The love redeems passions in the present underneath qualms which calm the sea. You can comment on all the questions that you have.

The rivers of love run free.

I am truly pleased with the way the mountains will give in to the passing of time.

Every moment becomes forever when you love, and everything is a song.

Through its pain, it undoes everything wrong.

You can be yourself, without purpose or despair, by bearing witness to your love.

LOVE WAS NOT ENOUGH FOR US

We were in love, but it was not enough.

It was not meant to be. We began on a well-worn road, but it wasn't.

We could not have been satisfied with the tenderness or delight that we felt despite years of anger and dissonance.

We were too different, our lives too distant.

You and I didn't get along very well, but put it aside

It was not until one day too late to reignite your heart.

The one who told her that she had finally died was astonished by the second.

Then, but then? We felt the pain of our loss.

The deepest and most unbearable sorrow.

We had to do it all by ourselves.

We would love to know how much we loved.

LOVERS ARE NOT ALWAYS THE BEST FRIENDS

Love isn't the same as friendship:

Sometimes, too much lies in their bed sheets. They need someone to help them share their sweets and sorrows from a relationship that will always end.

The marriage of friendship and love is a true sign of lasting love.

Compassion is what ignites the fire in others.

It's you I confide in most. You are the inner ear that I speak to all day.

When I'm home, I feel like I live in a different world.

It is also my joy to see the pleasure you find in me. The quiet delight, comfort and ecstasy that I give you are my gifts.

IT IS EASY TO LOVE YOU

It is easy to love you. Like walking through the sun listening to music.

You can find reasons to do something when you are ready. I don't care if the days at work are dull.

It's not worth it and there are many long hours. I am strong because you love me, and the light inside me lets me live clearly. Love is the meaning of life.

What is the lilt of our work that justifies our existence? The beauty no platitude could ever describe.

You are a gift that has been stopped in its act.

There's always a moment of joy.

I LOVE YOU MORE THAN HEAVEN

I have more love in my heart that heaven, angels, God and all the saints combined, can ever contain.

Even though we are apart, you're in my garden. I touch you while Time transforms into gold.

What if we could not bring back our beloved Eden?

Enjoy pleasures that are far greater than the dreams you've been told.

MY LOVE IS SOMETHING SEPARATE

What we do or say is not my love.

Even though we may have a disagreement, I still love you.

As waves pass by the rocky shoreline on their way,

Even if they know what is coming, keep going.

No matter what happens, I'll come.

Break against the wilderness, and beyond all pain.

I FEEL THE NIGHT ALL DAY LONG

The night comes all day and closes the external door.

But I still stay.

It is easier to miss you.

I'd rather suffer through missing your thoughts than that. So I would rather endure through.

It is better to suffer than to be empty.

Even though you're not here, I still want to have You with me. Your light is the one that gets me through the night, but brings darkness wherever I go.

NO MATTER WHAT OUR TROUBLES, I STILL LOVE YOU

Even though we have had our problems, I love you as if you were a part me.

It's not easy to live, but without you I will have bitterness.

The broken heaven is in my heart.

Darkness under all art and time,

There's nothing to hide about the pain. When we met for the first time, our love was so strong.

The sea is a river. Do not allow despair to turn into regret.

Love has chosen us. We can be what we choose to be. Love cannot last without will.

If we had to walk through a desert, I would still love you.

OUR LOVE IS TORN BY MILES, NOT BY CHOICE

We are not separated by distance, but by our own choice. My darling, you'll see me soon. Your voice and body are my instruments at night.

Soon, the tears and hands will belong to you. You're my dream, and I wish I could love you for all those hours that we have missed.

You're everywhere in my head. I'm afraid that my desire for you will be so strong, it could overwhelm the reality. Time must also temper our touch, so love can again be free and slow.

I'm already half-crazy with excitement; soon, my body will devour its treasure.

OUR LOVE'S A PLACE WHERE I NO LONGER LIVE

It's no longer a place I live. That used to be a home and is now just a building. The other day I went into my heart.

I didn't recognize anything in it as mine.

It's strange how the world changes and that what we love becomes something else in our hands.

Later, as we struggle to understand it, the light of our tears will fade.

On a bright morning I was awake to the sound of what I thought would be music. It was yesterday that I remembered, as if it had been a few years ago.

PASSION MAY REMAIN A GIFT

Love isn't free. Passion can be a present.

Two must be given to love and love someone else, or love will not be.

The decision to love is made every single day. To overcome the mountains, two people must work together.

When two people act together, they can break down the walls between them and me.

Love in everyday life will be as pure and ecstatic, just like love's pure ecstasy.

Create sweet, green stone fields.

MAYBE IT IS TOO EARLY FOR A REVEAL

It's too soon to love a feeling that isn't ready.

It is true that the light at dawn, however hesitant it may be, will come to pass. The doubts and joy that mingle with fear are what I carry as I dance through the fields of my heart. When we are apart, I am only half of myself. All I desire is to be with you when you are near.

PLEASE DON'T MIND IF I MAKE LOVE TO YOU

Imagine another person in my arms.

Anyone will do, no one is special

Her charms haven't been sanitized by her claims. The lust of power is more powerful than love.

The act of buying someone by the hour.

The love of giving is more important than lust: Yes, pleasure, but passion fades slowly.

Yes, there is affection, but we need more: the knife-sharp edge that lust betrays. My love, give me the flesh to fuel the dream. As I do for you. That lust may love redeem.

THE PRECISE POLITICAL PARTIES

We are afraid to love.

We sentimentalize, buried trivialities become treasure.

It was a real boredom.

What is the fantasy that carries death and suffering, awakening winter's wind?

What if we lived an ecstasy that ripped apart our joys, leaving behind what we loved on wings, winds and chains?

PRETEND THIS POEM IS ME, AND I AM WITH YOU

Imagine that this is you, I'm with you. I will hold you within the circle of fire.

Join me at my root and all time and space will disappear.

You are with me in a room that I have created for you. I shut the door, and I take you into my arms.

You are my body, I, and my world until I return to my lonely sleep.

The miles between us are no longer a problem. We can still make love, even if we're not physically together.

Your passion and hope for me is greater than any other man I may meet.

PROVERBS OF LOVE

One can suffer alone, but in order to truly be tormented one needs to love.

Love is more difficult to give than accept.

To love fully is to embrace both death and life. Love fully means to accept both life and death.

The secret to happiness is easy: Love, give, and care.

Why are there so many people unhappy? They are scared.

You are only loved if you love yourself.

If you love only your family, then they are all alone. If you love only your family then your family will be alone.

If you love only your country, then your nation will be alone. Love of God is the only way to achieve communion with oneself and God.

WHO SAID IT WAS EASY?

Who said that it is easy to maintain old flames?

Sometimes even experts need a bit of divine guidance.

It is easy to be Shakespearean.

It's much harder to be someone else's light.

Love, for example, requires more than just fuel.

The most dangerous leap is the one into your lover's mind.

The miracle of remaining in love during the long, icy agony

Anger?

The desire for freedom is only slightly greater than the fear of it.

Love is not a desire, but a fear.

No one would be able to keep the fire going

It is not the most wonderful, sweetest and best thing we have ever experienced.

TAKE IT AS A GIVEN
THAT I LOVE YOU

It is a fact that I am in love with you.

Let the conversation continue from there. Tell me how to get you to care.

What makes you dislike me? Tell me why.

Why you need to insist on loving me when you can't stand the amount I love.

Truth is deeper than what we think, and reaches regions that are not even in our minds. Opinions rarely disturb needs.

Love does not give advice until it is asked for. Take a plunge in yourself like a wave.

Tell me what you really want from me.

TELL ME MORE, MY LOVE, HOW MUCH YOU LOVE ME

You love me, tell me. When I'm hungry, give me a kiss to cool me down.

You should never hide your fascination. I am not perfect, but sometimes, you may find me to be. Of course, you may also ask me the same.

You will inspire me to have the same dedication if you do not put anything in your life before me.

Lovers can only find their happiness in this way.

THANK YOU FOR STAYING IN MY LIFE

Thank you for being in my life.

How could I possibly have sent you on your way? **I might not have paid for my sins; another person may well be responsible.** My sweet revenge is a result of the bitterness in my heart. Kindness in all you do.

You must really love me to remain. In bidden I'm grateful to have you.

THE RISK OF PAIN IS EQUAL TO THE CHANCE OF HAPPINESS

Chances of happiness are equal to the risks of pain. It's impossible to believe that you can love someone.

It's more true than you think

You won't know until it disappears. The sea of time is where you cut, but it roils on what you left behind.

My love is singing in the stars or hissing against the rocks, like the ocean.

When you stop to mourn, unravel your life. Returning in the sunshine, or with the rain.

THE DIFFERENCE BETWEEN LOVE AND LUST

What is the difference between love, and lust? Love is all about you.

I am a woman who is enamoured with me.

THE FIRST TRUE SIGN OF LOVE IS ANGER

First, anger is a sign of true love. We resent what we want.

The white stone is no longer standing alone. Fear of the finis.

It produces a deeper shimmering of sublime.

A subterranean scream is ushered in by a sunny, delicate malaise.

No one can be bent and still turn back.

Every part of the self is a stranger.

OUR EMBRACE IS UNBARRED

Our embrace is unbounded, and our presence in the heart is more powerful than any bar. Our lives are filled with grace and love, even though we're still separated.

There is no more powerful presence than the one in your heart. No more poignant touch than that of a vision. Still together, but still apart

It is more fortunate than it seems.

There is no touch that can be more important than a wish, though sometimes dreams are all you need. It is more fortunate than it seems

You can only trust me if I also trust you.

Even though dreams are sometimes all we have, our life is filled with grace and love.

No barriers can separate us if I and you both trust each other.

THERE ARE SOME PLEASURES I WOULD TRY WITH YOU

You know, there are some things I'd like to try out with you. They are so sweet that I can't tell you.

The dark is a more romantic view for those who love each other

Words or light can often ruin things. Close your eyes, let go and allow me to guide you blindly into ecstasy.

Let the desire flow through your doors

My tongue could show me every orifice. Beauty is not the master of one sense but of all. Inner eye: Awaken to a more complex aesthetic

Your cry will reveal more than sight can. Join me to enjoy the beauty of the night.

Touch becomes our eye, love is our light.

THERE IS NO LIFE WITHOUT ITS SHARE OF PAIN

You cannot love without feeling pain.

You must be in a state of mind, but you cannot.

No aspirin or cure for sadness exists.

You will meet new friends and lovers

Then, pass through the death of faithlessness or by death.

If you want to live in happiness, then embrace your pain. All you need and love will be destroyed by time, but you can love tomorrow.

THE TRUTH IS RARELY AN EXPRESSION OF LOVE

The truth is not always a sign of love. Honesty often comes before pain.

Romance is best when it's a little confused.

But lies will eventually suck passion out.

If one wants to be loved, then it is important to tell the truth. Not in a cruel way but just enough to dispel delusion.

Every love has to be broken and then rebuilt.

WE MET AS MERELY WORDS UPON A SCREEN

The only thing we met was words on a screen. Disembodied spirits who have found love

By the mind and unrecognized yearning.

The best thing about falling in love was that we didn't even have to see each other.

The words that burn are two hidden fires, which can sate hunger better than any feast or flesh.

The majority of people are influenced by their sight, and they love what needs to be changed most urgently.

We took steps we didn't plan, On a passionate, sure path.

WE MET UPON THE INTERNET

The friendship began on the internet

Inevitably, platonic expression is expressed by words or thoughts alone.

It is impossible for us to meet in person because we live far apart.

Our feelings and hearts are much closer than family.

You are your dearest self, without a face or voice.

You can find us in our own cyberspace.

WE STARTED OUT AS

FRIENDS AND NOW IT'S LOVE

It started as friendship and has now become love. It's beautiful that you can move around so effortlessly.

This is pure gain. No rough edges. The turn I took was not something that I had planned, There were no maybes or possibly.

I had a desire for love, but it was never mine until I felt the heart of friendship moving. Never before have had I felt more at home.

So rich is my life now. You can now enjoy my pleasure, and I will do the same for you. Never did I think that it would be my only life.

I flitted around like a ghost, looking in at other peoples' doors.

WHAT MAKES STARS ROMANTIC?

What is romantic about stars? What makes stars romantic?

What about the blue-white throng of witnesses staring back at you in silence?

What about the eternal fascination? (For love

It is a piece of eternity lodged within the heart.

Why two when only one is so little? Is it the desire to be touched in a temple? It is the vast and lonely field of life where love too shines.

Amidst darkness? There are so many people who love each other.

Is it passion in a celebrity's heart or is there something else? Love's heat illuminating the emptiness.

What does the ardor of a star hurling across light-years of pain tell us about its inner yearning?

WHEN AT THE SAME TIME, ONE FEELS JOY AND SORROW

Sunlit sorrow weeping golden tearless, when one is simultaneously filled with joy and sadness.

Happy today but cautious of tomorrow. Half consumed by pride, half by tears.

Riche in happiness, but knows one will soon lose fortune.

But poor for that which one does not want; when the sun is in full glory.

It must meet its unwelcome end, then one has to find beauty in their story and, as the sun never stops, let the light shine. Till you return home, I will do the same.

Feel this joy despite my pain.

WHEN WE BROKE UP, YOU SAID THAT YOU'D ALWAYS LOVE ME

You said that you would always love me. You said that we would always be friends.

Then I realized that this is the end.

It's easier to tell a lie when you say, "Oh, this is harder than I expected."

It was a nice gesture, but I wasn't brave enough to ask the reason.

Why we've failed doesn't really matter, nor does why I still love you after everything you've done.

Why the truth must be revealed after the last train is gone.

Even though I hate you, I still love you.

I cannot know what happened.

YOU ARE EVERYTHING I EVER WANTED

You are all I've ever wanted.

On you my future happiness depends.

Unless you're with me, my mind is haunted.

After seeing you, I feel more at ease. **R**eason warns that I'm in danger. **R**eason fades away.

Like your lovely is also flammable when angry.

I am not afraid because my trust in you is so great. There's something more to our love than emotions, **underneath every thought and desire is**. Not even the entire ocean of water can contain all that we feel.

Is a small but effective firefighting tool.

What could it be? There is something within our love.

Immeasurable and infinite.

Nothing can compare to this in the world of life

If it were possible, each other passion could be.

YOU DON'T LOVE ME, BUT AH! DO I LOVE YOU?

But you don't really love me. Do I love you!

I hate that you've got another one! Every day, I am entertained by the antics and humor of your two happy hopping birds. You are as tethered to me as a fish is to the sea.

As the sun is to Earth, or as the moon is to Earth. It is so painful to think of letting it go that I'd rather just let the pain run.

If I keep waiting, I will have you. This love must be able to break down all barriers! Your natural light will continue to shine until the rotation of your day turns into night. This sorrow will last until then:

The source of my pain must be the hope for joy.

YOU HAD ME FOR A NIGHT, THEN TURNED

AWAY

Then you turned me away. You inspired a love that was not yours.

You might not be able to unenchant me.

Show yourself you can have it your way.

Now I am left with the guilt of love. That took unashamed pleasure in your happiness. You treated me like a fake, sexual toy.

What I thought was not important to me.

It's the worst that I crave your touch.

It's your irritation that drives me crazy! Knowing how badly I have been cheated makes me mad!

It does not make me less interested in you.

YOU HAVE AN ANGEL'S FACE, A LOVING HEART

Your face is like an angel, and you have a heart of love. You smile with a peaceful sunlit glow that will last forever. The whole is you, and I am only a small part.

There is another world that exists beyond love. Such thoughts are just poetry. When I think of you, however, it's impossible to remove my thoughts.

You can feel the glow of my inner being.

What a happy and happy life it is to have a tender feeling like if he lit a candle in your eyes.

You'll always be the true heart of my life, like a bright sun gliding across my sky.

YOU LEFT ME, BUT YOU CANNOT LEAVE MY HEART

My heart is not yours to leave. You are still in my heart, whether you want to be or not. You will always be a part of me.

You'll hear about the pain and suffering I experience.

You've hurt me and made me bleed. You will remember your cold words.

Give me the comfort I need. The real problem is that I cannot solve it alone.

The real you is far away from my reach. Since my real intention is to steal The You I Loved, the true you isn't very much. I'll be gentle with you:

You left me a lovely memory.

YOU WROTE YOUR NAME ON HER THIGH

You wrote her name on the thigh and looked me in the eye. Why did You do that to me? What evil demon made You so different from you?

You seem to want to make Me feel bad, almost as if you were testing the depth of my grief

See how sweet the pain is that You must feel to be alive.

Love is a scary thing. I'm afraid of it.

My role is to repeatedly prove that you can't lose

You want something but you can't choose it.

You can never be both fully loved AND fully free. Love is mutual.

YOU'RE LIKE MUSIC PLAYING IN MY HEAD

It's like I hear music in my head every day.

It's not knowing what to say or where I am that I think about you when I open a door. I am in an embrace that never ends.

I hug the sweet idea that you're mine. While walking through a park, I care not if it's sunny or rainy. Our love must be new, because it can't continue like this forever.

You must also take into consideration other matters

I will clear out my mind of all smiles, tears and gratitude. Such talk is a fantasy for me.

You are the world, but you're not.

YOUR FEAR IS NOT SURPRISING

It's not surprising that you are afraid. The end is always bad:

Fury, betrayals, recriminations.

For days, weeks and even months there was an agony that was worse than grief

You also think you are a complete fool.

The love you feel is similar to diving or climbing rocks: It's spectacular, but it sticks in your throat every moment.

It's easy to be careless, and it makes you feel loose in your stomach.

As love nears, the knot becomes tighter like a serpent.

Looking in on the world from outside is similar to being alone and free:

When people give affection they also receive it.

You can live in hell and prison,

Work out what you need to do.

You can watch the videos as though they are on television.

Love and difficulties are part of life.

You cannot get to its riches without making a choice. It is only possible to enter by adoring this or that individual. People will always fall short of what you hope for.

It is impossible to love and live without being loved.

It's the same as spending all your life in your bedroom.

YOUR HEART BROKE WHEN I SAID I HAD TO LEAVE YOU

You were devastated when I told you I would have to leave for a far-off place in order to serve my country.

Every day I tell you how much I care for you and how I will make it right once I am home.

Life is but a fantasy, and dreamers like us, make what we want of who we are.

We are the ones who redeem ourselves when gates close. Love leaves a door open for us.

Dream with me as we search for ways to still be together during these months of sadness.

Dreams and longings are not more certain than the strength of our will.

ROMANTIC POEMS

THE RIGHT TIME, THE RIGHT WAY

Need someone to help me?

You were the one I was looking for.

With anticipation, but with doubt

Your grace and softness touched me.

You responded well to my request and need with your presence.

I was glad you came.

When you came, it was the perfect time.

The right way.

SPEAK TO ME OF LOVE AND MORE

The first time I saw you.

I was able to see something extraordinary

Between us, with you and in you

The first time I saw you I felt special.

We were special.

Answer me now and get a free strip

Your image is it the echo of what I want?

You can tell me about such things and more.

By eyes that are bright as candles and unarming coy smiles around lips so pure and virgin; by natural beauty unaffected by false disguises and spiritual energy flowing to your talents for the future; and through a life so full of confidence, yet modestly true and unartificed.

This first-parting sweetness is it a Dream that you should keep or just a fleeting memory?

It's the Inspirer design that inspired the Inspirer

It will be a privilege to see you again, even if it is only a passing glance.

Your lovely face is aglow with a burgeoning Energy?

Sweet flower, speak to me and pray

You can smell and sense your fragrance again by chance.

Your natural vibrancy.

It could be friendship, or even more.

It is the spiritual meeting of two souls who love each other so much that they want to share themselves with the world.

I FEELS I KNOW YOU

Sometime I think I have been transported to another planet; other times I believe I can see a whole new world.

Some days I think I have stood with you in the same space; this moment and space of our first meeting.

The meeting of the eyes

It was as if I already knew you; it felt as if I always wanted you.

You are mine, even though I tried to fight my desire for you.

Come to me with burning desire and peace, let's be one. I have waited for you across many lifetimes.

The parade of many

Let us come and savor our souls from our past lives, as we fulfill our long-lasting dreams.

We invite you to come to our table to enjoy the energy of each other.

You can teasingly smirk at Dessert as you face me;

Do not rush to the sacred sensuality in our long Romance sleep;

My love, please come to me.

FIRST GLIMPSE - FIRST DANCE

Your face was the first thing I saw, and it took my gaze to your core;

You and I both knew we were made for one another.

When I first touched you, it was clear that you had been Sculpted into my embrace. We glided together in the musical magic movement to our spirits' call.

We danced so effortlessly, and with such pleasure that we were like playful birds in flight and our energies breathed to the life of real memories and a living energy.

Thank you for dancing, sweet lady

Let me hold you again to our spiritual rhythm

Unending music

WILL YOU COME WITH ME?

Your image is what I am seeking

You are my ideal woman, even though I don't know you exist.

Please come along with me.

Share your life with me;

Together, we'll create life and be a trustee of another.

Bring me along and I'll pick you a red Hibiscus

The sweet magnolia is the fragrance of your perfume.

The stars will watch over us as long as you and
I live.

ROMANTICA

We meet again in the air that unites us.
To breathe in the anticipation of possible love,
our private space is where I want to be.

Your fresh flower has sprung forth from the tender buds of youth, luring my patience and long-awaited wisdom.

Face to you I focus my energy on the field of spirit; wanting to be near you to feel your eyes and arms, but not too soon to ruin the pleasure of our precious urges.

Your reservation should not betray the future of an entire love between two people.

Our moments of sensual desire.

Let's have a romantic evening together, combining sparkling drinks with rhythmical dancing, and musical songs under the stars.

The full moon, the colorful flowers, and pastel towels.

Let me veil you under the most pure Lace, allowing your eyes to shine through.

Touch your lips gently and slowly, to forever seal the romance of our union.

Love is a precious thing.

We will go patiently in the direction of fate's call,

And we will have sweet memories of our dreams coming true.

Create we will two or more lives.

A Romance will always endure, despite the trials of life.

Come with me, I will be there with you

Let our love grow anew, and pierce deeply within our hearts an untarnished commitment.

The sacred message:

ROMANTICA, ROMANTICA, ROMANTICA!

A WEDDING PLEDGE

This is my right hand. I am taking you to be my wife/husband.

And will hold your life sacred as long as we are together.

Pick up and hold one another;

My right hand is my promise that I will work with you and you for the sake of our life together.

With both my hands I nurture the Trust we have in each other and ourselves, as partners in life.

This heart declares my commitment to your needs and wants, but not to anyone else's.

It is with determination and will that I promise to be Patient and understanding with you, your flaws and your changes over the years.

I am confident You will also do so with me.

You will always be in my thoughts and I'll share experiences whenever possible.

In this moment, I promise to do everything I can.

Forgive you of your inadvertent mistakes due to human weakness.

Respect you both as a human being and my husband/wife. Be open about my feelings and thoughts.

You are my morning kiss and nightly touch.

You can trust your words and actions.

Respect your freedom and privacy.

Individuality,

I am totally committed to our relationship.

Furthermore,

I'll do my very best to not hurt You in any way, or make you look bad before others or myself;

You will find inner peace and growth.

No one will be able to make me lose my love for You. I won't allow false feelings for someone else or the many exciting things in life to blind me.

You can talk to me, I'll walk with you and we will persevere through all the tests and conditions;

You can count on me to pray, believe, and struggle for you.

The most important thing is that I love you unconditionally for as long as I am able and you wish me to.

Hope and Trust that it will last forever.

HOLIDAY

It's a holiday to celebrate culture; but it doesn't matter the differences

Our worlds are far apart

We must celebrate this Merry Day of Glee -- our love for ourselves;

It's not our holiday.

It's a time to love and celebrate the happiness of special people.

LET'S WRITE A SCRIPT WITHIN OUR HEART

Write a play in your heart and let's act it out.

Spontaneity is the ability to react in the moment;

Reduce our drive, let us feel and realize what we need.

Our anxieties subdued, our depression minimized;

Enjoy your loved ones and

Enjoy the world around you;

We can eat together, relax, go exploring, and have a conversation in each other's presence.

Security, comfort, and good company;

Write a story from the moment to moment in our hearts.

In our lives.

WE SAW IN EACH OTHERS' EYES

We sat alone,
We drank wine,

No intellectualized thought was given to the subject.

We then saw in each other's eyes the true nature of who we are.

We realized that we were women.

We then communicated nonverbally our desire to move towards our partner.

We suppressed our desire as we lowered the volume of our instruments.

We have a fascination for our tools,

Our rational being is slowly destroyed by our passions.

The cloak that hid us is gone.

Honey from each other's fruit can bring out the true selves.

CAN I BE FREE WITH YOU?

You can be yourself with me.

You don't have to hurry, you don't have to prove or be anything.

Can you and I both be ourselves?

Can we all be together, one?

LET ME LOVE YOU IN THE MORNING OF YOUR WOMANHOOD

Let me into your heart

The clay that your parents made will be a great
help to me;

I will touch your morning years of womanhood
and transform you.

Let me be your next heart.

The warmth from your breath will be a great
pleasure to mine and stroke.

Please massage my ears, so that I can feel the
life of yours grow within my arms and I might
live through it again.

Your life of love

You will be the lady of my night in all situations
and all time.

A FINE WOMAN

Let me be that woman with the straight neck and strong hips.

Let me feel the elegance of your space as I watch your poised presence and your poised position.

You are a beautiful woman with tanned skin and a creamy texture.

I am secretly watching you, patiently waiting for my chance to meet you.

Visualize your beautiful essence and feel your tranquil temperament.

On this special night, I want to give you my full attention.

We will dine together under the stars in this resort, and we'll smile at each other.

As the night turns to dawn, let us be one in our moment and space.

THE MEANING OF ROMANTIC LOVE

Two dynamos are a romantic love when they
turn on each other and feed into one another;

Total energy is directed towards another, which
makes one lose track of time and space.

The romantic love that is a contradiction to
reality and responsibility, as well as obscuring
it, contradicts the rationale and obscures its
understanding.

This is a fantasy that has been acted out for the
moment and hoped forever.

The romantic love between two people is when
they are the only ones in the world who value
each other and their essence at all times.

The visceral thrill is what drives you to fulfill
your capacity for Sensitivity and Possibility;

The romantic love that provides a sense of
security and enhances the worldly.

The appreciation of physical and mental health,
as well as the promotion of confidence;

The force is what drives the people to their
knees, pushes them up a level in emotional
realization, and overwhelms all human control.

The essence of romantic love is to give for the sheer joy of it, share with the other person just because you want to, and enjoy each other simply because they are there.

WAIT FOR A CALL

This date I have lived from morning to night.

It would be nice to hear you again, across the miles.

You've promised to call me to finish my day and make it special.

You are the only one in this night's solitude.

This day I have lived in anticipation of Your tone of the phone's call.

You alone.

It's been a long day for me to just hear your breath and sigh.

You can call me.

You've been saying that to me all day.

I love you.

NOSTALGIC
LOVE POEMS

OUR LAST NIGHT TOGETHER

We stood in the moonlight on a night.

The pit was never explored under the cover of the backyard tree.

Our youthful lava-like desires last night.

The eve was a night of caress and we stood there for hours.

The moving truck was coming and we counted our last moments together, ever, so painfully.

Her miniature chain and cross were placed in my hands as a sign of memory; she only watched me.

Clutch it passionately, before I lose it in my jeans pocket.

When her father said "bedtime", she gave one final hug and a last kiss.

She walked reluctantly away and shielded her.

This treacherous entrance from the torment of night lights;

Her back was beautifully lit by the moonlight as she turned around to show me her last face.

WE WALKED

The sun-baked earth and our shoes powdered up.

As we walked so close to each other, oblivious of our schoolmates.

We both 15, she 13 years old, and we are all innocents and timid.

Yet our feelings have been awakened by maturity.

As we touched the voice and face of our partner, there was no kiss.

Our own young Company has ears that are so tuned, and eyes that are so focused.

We used to enjoy a walk in the afternoons, which we looked forward to every morning.

LOVE ME NOT WITH WORDS ONLY

Your voice is so sweet and laudatory.

Your mirror eye should sparkle and shine.

It will complement the tone of your voice.

You vibrations are good news for me. I love to hear positive news.

The sounds are sweet, but they're so transient.

You can't love me with just words.

You can show me that you love me by your actions.

By action, sacrifice, and effort;

Share time and eat together

Take a bite under a tree in summer, dance in front of everyone, and hold hands with synchronized steps.

We must all work, play, and plan together to protect our own lives, as well as those of others.

It is good to laugh together, meditate with each other, suffer together and have fun together.

You can love me by giving your full feelings, thoughts, and actions.

You can't love me with just words.

I'M GLAD I MET YOU

Gee, I'm glad I met you;

We have all become better together;

You have been sharing with each other.

Our sensations have been realized; we have felt reality.

The two of us have shared feelings and knowledge.

We've also encountered the worlds of each other.

The mere presence of another has increased our joys and minimized our pain;

Gee, I'm glad I met you;

Remember all of the pleasant and good times we have had together.

Let's reserve each other a place in our hearts.

All those precious moments and special memories.

LET US MAKE MEMORIES

Make memories we can treasure forever

Make them up in your mind of spontaneous and planned experiences about yourself

All the seasons of Earth and their splendor.

Let us breath in spring, fall or by the water, whether it is in a park, a waterfront or if we are at the beach.

Romantic feelings and thoughts are the energies that surround us.

Make memories we can appreciate today but cherish forever in our hearts.

WOULD YOU ROW IN MY BOAT?

Sit in my boat when the fog is thickest.

The Coolness of dawn protects virgin love's innocence and Goodness.

Sit with your face facing mine

Let the sun shine brightly and reveal the beauty of the eyes, skin and lips.

Come and sit down with me.

Let our love gently disturb my favorite flowery dress from our first meeting.

I LONG FOR YOU

Relax now!

The privacy of your temple is not what I desire, but the whole of you.

To be with you at anytime and anywhere.

Your Energy, your Respect and your presence would make me better.

Enjoyment and gratitude are a worthy reward.

You will be able to tell my motives and cause.

Sincerely I yearn for your soul, heart, presence, and warmth.

NOSTALGIA II

The night was lit up brightly.

The two of us stood under the table, looking down at our toes.

You gently touched me with your breath and I felt a surge of warmth within.

I am confined by the tremors of my shyness.

The night was lit up brightly.

How I miss the cooling breeze

The midnight air which swept us back home; you touched my hand using your fingers

We shook our hands in stride.

We pacing onwards, but so slowly.

The night was bright and our youth tortured us.

Consent thought of the passing time.

The night was dark, but we were still in each other's private world.

No further attention was paid to the matter.

The night was lit up brightly.

It seemed to us that it would never fade.

NOSTALGIA III

This was an era to be remembered

Romance galore and memories of unforgettable adult images that are seen through the eyes of children;

The time was when black shoes shone, and hats of fine quality were so beautiful;

Men's tie and coat

The romantic dance of women with their stockings raised high.

The navy blue gabardine trousers;

The hard work was not rewarded.

Every day, we offer nightly prayers to show our appreciation.

In June and December things were simple. People had more time and energy to love.

When people were at peace and had the time to think,

QUINTINA

You see, there was a girl named Quintina.

The smile on the face of an 8-year old child who is bright and cheerful;

The girl grew into a woman after years of her absence

Beautiful woman or a lady of fine appearance;

You have the courage to act with class and elegance.

She showed a sweet feminine face;

Quintina smile to the whole world; Quintina please smile once more for me.

LIE DEAD

Relax and enjoy the peace of the sea.

You ear

Allow the sand to tickle you back, and let the sun wash your face.

We should only think about our own feelings and the moment we are in.

Let the air of life bring us meaning so that we can breathe in such memories forever.

WEAR WHITE DRESS FOR ME

It's for you, in the sundown of your womanhood.

Memory of innocence and coy

We can all relate to the spontaneity and innocence of private moments.

I can see myself wearing it in my head.

The old oak trees shaded by the sun and the images of the sunshine.

Wear me a white gown in the sundown of your womanhood, so I can see the purest form of my love.

You will be the temple of my everlasting and unwavering trust.

SENSUAL
LOVE POEMS

WE LOVE - BEFORE WE LOVE

Washing each other's images is necessary before we can love the height of love.

To touch with care, to hear our partner's breath on the rest of the neck is what we should do.

Before we fall in love and love's peak, we should romance the other.

SHE CAME AT 5

He washed her in his likeness at twelve and brought her to him at five.

Her natural fragrance told of the day's work.

The mixture which roused the Heaven that he had so eagerly awaited;

Love will greet you from four walls; touch it, embrace the energy of your sweetest wish,

Your fondest thought, His most cherished dream, and His only source of living;

The lady is his woman.

THE LOVE HAS COME

The way he treated her was so gentle.

She was brave, but also filled with a deep sense of exhilaration that she had never felt before.

The two were united in their ecstasy on top of a mountain.

Together they discovered a shyness.

Separation is awkward and downhill. However, the dream has been fulfilled.

She relaxed on her arm, and he leaned against the softness of his;

She whispered in his ear.

He replied "I also love you."

WILL YOU TOUCH ME?

Too long since I last saw you;

Will you kiss me tenderly with your fingertips aglow?

And feel the warmth of the past love.

What if we could free our Passion spirit?

You can touch me in this moment, the secret space of love that we share today, so that together,

We may continue to live our lives as once.

Walk slowly to me and come.

You are so much larger in my view. I will embrace you wholeheartedly.

Too long since I last saw you

Will you and I touch each other as we did before?

POETICA SENSEROTICA

She spoke about the passion of love:

"Come within me, dear love.

Let my love for you only penetrate deep to your tip

Let me come to you as your soul yearns for me

As peacefully as the lamb, to your passionate lion growls and sweet sensual satisfaction;

"Let me feel, touch and breathe the celebration and acclamation of our romantic love."

He replied:

I will be waiting for you, my one and only love.
And enter the chamber of love.

I will lay on you the long held Desire, and
release the tension in love that is needed to
bring forth the hidden orchids.

Let me be the sound of your kitten purring and
the gentle touch of a lion to the tender side of
your loin.

In this love life, we want to be able to feel our
souls and hearts ablaze, forever.

"And in the love of your life, remain."

YOUR PURSUIT IS MY PURSUIT

My pleasure to you, dear love.

It is my light.

You will be able to burn the chains of joy loose
by sharing the desires you inspire in me.

Your most valuable and irreplaceable reservoir
of sensations.

Now is the time to act, now!

Come into our arms and let's set the honey we have made ablaze.

Fruits that have been ripened.

Our romantic desire and future happiness can be trusted in this spiritual and natural attraction.

I WANT YOU

The unforeseen was not the reason we sat together;

We touched our eyes out of politeness,

but they were quickly locked by the magnetic pull Of their own vibrations.

The two of us struggled with our emotions and trembled in an attempt to sequester and control them.

We filled our eyes with each other in subtlety and conciseness between the interludes of trying to appear unassuming.

The scent of our genders revealed the desire in our deep breathes; our skin was flinching and muscles were tense.

While we were waiting for different buses and hoping that they wouldn't be late this time; we parted painfully knowing

We would see each other soon, but wondering so desperately.

When and how?

LOVE BONE'S WISH

I will explore the sites and let you feel my tender love bone tip.

Your hidden love is asleep in the honey-colored chamber of your darkest secret.

I will awaken your deepest feelings.

The heights and depths of life are two connected things.

This love moment is a whole idea;

Your bones will embrace me with my heart bone

Our irresistible love in a moment and an experience.

POEMS ON
LOVE LOST

TO SAY "HELLO" IS TO SAY "GOOD-BYE"

Saying "hello", is saying "goodbye."

It's the way things work; faces appear in winter and disappear in spring. Doors are opened to be shut.

Sun rises and sun sets

All people will laugh and cry when babies come, and as old folks pass away.

The moon follows the day as night naturally follows.

The same way that hatred can steal away the promise of love, boredom takes from us our excitement in life.

Enjoy, Excite, and Appreciate the "Hello".

You can say "goodbye" to your loved ones without any anger, sadness, or grief.

It's normal to greet someone by saying "hello."

LOVE KNOCKED

When love knocked, you refused.

When love knocked on your door, you opened it;

The awry feelings of joy and pain;

The tension and conflict between pleasure and pain; and the peaks and valleys of sensual sweetness; you called,

Love shut the door.

You called twice and Love replied, "No more."

DON'T PASS ON LOVE

The love that is lost can never be found again.

Love can be unmade by a choice that is delayed;

If you think too much about love, you may be misunderstanding the opportunity for love.

Then;

If you grieve for a long time about the loss of a beloved, you will be suffering daily on your own.

Precious cost;

If you wait too long to find the perfect prince or princess, life may leave you empty-hearted.

You can regret a missed opportunity

Follow your feelings

You're less likely to be caught up in your own thoughts because of a love you passed on.

It is only your fault.

Your regret will be a love that you have missed.

LOSS

Losing is having had.

You cannot love and lose someone without falling in Love.

You can lose your spouse or child even if you have never been married.

Creation or adoption of life.

The images or experiences of that person will never be lost.

It is possible to lose the presence of a beloved, but not their memories.

Losing is the same as having.

TODAY AND TOMORROW

Today is a happy day!

Today is the best; tomorrow will be sad.

Today, you will be rejected tomorrow.

Good-bye tomorrow; Here today,

The life we know is gone tomorrow.

POETIC WORDS TO MY LOVE

You will never be seen again.

Recall our happy times together;

You will always be in my heart and mind if I have to leave today or tomorrow.

Your call has not been deferred in times of crisis;

The promise I made was not kept

Unfulfillable;

Remember: If God wills that I never see you again on this earth, please remember to keep the following in mind.

You were my first love,

You are my love, now and forever

You will be my forever love

LOVE IS LIKE CANDLE LIT

The love is like a lit candle

This is a burning, sometimes bright, other times dull, dim.

It is sometimes flickering, unsteady and pacing into darkness.

The love is like a lit candle

The glow of the sun

It casts its light to the skies, its warmth is spread by gentle breezes and it bolsters confidences through hopes of happiness.

It is love that makes a candle glow.

Burning;

Even though the candle of love may one day be a fading memory, it will always remain in our hearts.

It is important to cherish and enjoy every moment.

SICK LOVE

Tell me,

No love

Love is not death; it's only slavery.

Romeo and Juliet, or Othello and Desdemona

No love

If you are not in love,

Or a love betrayed, Or a love paid;

No love

Love of the body alone, or repeated anger and destruction;

No love

A love sickening.

WHEN PIECES FALL APART

As pieces break apart, the whole is no longer there.
Hurt, it hurts but keep going

With a deep love for those remnants,

we must cry. We should be moved by the priceless memory of past places, times, and people.

Do dry.

DEAR LOVE

It was stated:

"Dear love,

You can be sure I won't

You can call me or I will call you back.

I have nothing to ask for and nothing I need from you.

I am sorry that I did not appreciate what you shared with me, but I do not regret it.

Privacy of my absence

"And we both go our separate ways in search of our happiness."

GET TO KNOW

Knowing is missing, to have is not knowing.

The ecstasy Of Sensuality Is the Pain of Absence.

The love comes and goes.

Choose carefully, in couplets, its beneficiaries and victims, both of pain and joy, happiness and shame.

The beauty that comes and goes, of stars, flowers and theater lights, is amazing.

The love that comes and goes is the desire to have it.

LOVE WHAT YOU HAVE

If you can,

Once you lose it, you will miss what you love.

You will never be able love that person again.

Once you lose it, you will miss what you love.

You will not be able love it as much.

Once you lose it, you will miss what you love.

It is possible that you will never be able love someone else.

WILL YOU LOVE ME IF ...?

You'll love me even if I don't.

You will love me even if you are wrong.

You'll love me even if I don't?

What if you don't love me?

You will love me just as I am; will you love me even if my condition is paralyzed?

Will you still love me when I become lessened or embarrassed; will you stop loving me altogether?

What if I changed?

Will you still love me even if my ideals of what you find lovable have changed?

LIVE AGAIN

Do not die when another dies; do not die from the loss of a love or if a dream has gone wrong;

Do not grieve or regret anything;

Plan for the Future, Live Again, Look at the Present and Act in it;

You and those who depend on you must live again.

If you don't live now, you won't live long.

DIVORCE

The pain of love's Death is different from that caused by the death of an individual you love; it's a painful death.

The pain of the past is not forgotten by the buried tears of the future; the images of the wedding cake's reflection are recalled in the candle's glow, as well as the warmth of the child's eyes from an experience shared; the love gone awry In the shattered pieces of glass; the crushed crystal of the image of love lost to time.

The loss of love, separation and divorce are all cruel events.

The rare mixture of care, compassion, and hatred, a cauldron full of reflective thoughts, driven by the repeated pain of lost time and energy, sacrifices in sleep and food, and conscious hopes for revenge to defend hurt feelings, all in the name of self-satisfaction.

The loss of love, divorce, separation and physical pain.

Smiles have turned into frowns.

Promises are naught.

Pleasures become pain.

Yesterday's toast with wine glasses broken and wet.

Hopes scrawled on white tablecloth among vinegar-sour wine.

Fear of divorce, loss of love, separation and identity; doubts regarding self-confidence, trust and confidence;

The confused thoughts and hopes now blocked by the twisted heart are Love, still.

POEMS ON LOVE RESTORED

LOVE AGAIN

As you have fallen in love before, so too can you fall in love again.

More feeling, more care. Burn away the past.

The roots of enjoyment and learned memories are not to be found in the roots;

When you cap your grief and open up your heart, it is possible to love with faith.

You can hold the heat of romance as long as you breath air.

It is possible to love someone else.

You can love yourself as long you want.

CAN WE WAIT FOR THOSE THAT WE LOVE?

Why are you complaining?

All of us are waiting to die.

Why can't you wait to see those that we love?

You don't seem to mind that I am running late;
we all have to wait until death.

Why can't you wait to see those that we love?

WHAT IS LOVE ...?

What is Love?

What if not just for a time or a life?

What is Love?

What if it's not for the season -- or a feeling?

What is Love without the excitement;

It's not casting a magic spell

What is love without God's Spiritual sanction of
a divine Union between two meant to be one?

What is Love without God's spiritual sanction of
two people meant to become one?

HUG YOUR LOVE

If you feel anger or rage, hug your loved one.

If you feel anxiety or fear, hug your loved one.

If you are disappointed or unable to achieve your goals, hug those who love you.

If you are unsure or have reservations, hug your loved one.

If you feel pain, hug your loved one.

Hug your loved ones when there's a mutual sadness or joy.

Or simply just a moment to celebrate life.

Grab your loved one at dawn and bedtime.

LIVING AND LOVING ARE ARTS

Love is a form of living, and loving is a form of living.

It takes both thoughtfulness, not only thought.

Learning, not just performance.

Compassion, not just passion.

Not just care, but also concern.

Love life is living it with patience, respect and appreciation.

Love yourself, love others and live life.

Enjoying life to the fullest.

WE LAY

As we lay back, our eyes are aimed at the stars.

We think of nothing.

We will not forget the time of our gratitude.

As the darkness fell, we were shielded by the grass.

We are anonymous.

Our shared Presence was able to erase past regrets with the cool evening air

Worries about the future.

Our own breaths serenaded us and our thoughts about each other comforted us.

The two of us are really one.

Together, we can defeat the entire world.

HELLO I LIKE YOU

**Person 1
speaks:**

Please excuse me; hello

You were there;

You are a nice person;

"Would you like to speak?"

**Person 2
speaks:**

You are excused.

I'm also here, but not in my presence

You were also there;

You are welcome to talk to me too.

"I also like you."

LOVE'S CLAIM

We must let go of the past and the old images,
attitudes, and memories;

Start anew.

The Woman I Love is waiting for me.

I am the heart and soul of my manhood.

Come and claim my claim

The blood and Remains of My Life's Time;

The romance of our two hearts and my return
will be made easier.

Take the bad thoughts from your brow, And
claim back what was.

LOVE UNLOVED

Being deprived of someone you love is more
painful than not being with them.

Happiness is the result;

It is painful to "love One" you do not want to be
with and hope that you will one day make it.

You are free.

It is not romantic to live a lie from one kiss to the next, to cry in dull times, to laugh when you want to cry, and to be hopeless, to have a mind that cannot think straight, to smile when you wish to cry, and to cry when you desire to smile.

You can fill your life up with meaningful things.

You can fill your life's emptiness with the love you have regained, or seek new love by telling yourself truthfully.

OH WOMAN OH MAN

He asked, "Oh Woman," "How can you satisfy me?"

You are not able to think about our past love;

When I am tired of you displeasure and want the sweetness deeply,

Call to our memories of yesteryear; Spit out your bitter venom one time.

"For all and lay bare on my rose bed, Waiting for me to give you what pleasures are left of your unconscious Yearning."

She replied, "Oh my God," "How can you trust me?"

You can bring peace and calm to my thoughts by putting an end to doubts, rage, or apprehensions.

You can lie on your rose bed, I will.

"I feel so warm to the touch of your hands. I'm bared in yesterday's Ecstasy, but today we can enjoy the calm and peaceful peace that our Enlightened Romance has brought us."

LOVE'S HOPE RENEWED

The phrase is:

There is no shame and pain like the hurt and humiliation of Love Rejected;

It is confusing to have a love that you flaunt and then are not able to keep.

No cruelty can compare to the destruction of the spirit that a bad love or a once-loved has brought.

"There is no wish more lonely than that of the longing for the return a lost love."

With love's New Romance's Seeding its flowers and fruits are now in bloom.

The thoughts of Harvests past will be forgotten.

I LOVE TO WALK WITH ME

He said.

In my transition to a new love, I'm looking for a woman who will walk with me.

Behind me, to motivate me to become all that I can.

When I am honored for what she helped me become, I will need her to be there to support.

It is obvious that I will need someone to walk *in front of me*.

Help her become all that she is capable of becoming.

What I need is a - and that's all.

"Good woman, walk God's way in love with me and her.

I HAVE YOU AND YOU HAVE ME

If you have class, then there is no need to tell lies.

It's natural and you don't have to do anything;

Your eyes are bright like the supernova starlight that lights up the night sky.

It is not necessary to be concerned about your security.

Mental health is not a requirement to use drugs;

No need to be sad, you can enjoy happiness and peace;

It's like eating apple pie with sugar.

I'm yours and you don't have to say goodbye;

This poem is about you.

MATHEMATICAL LOVE

The number of true love, or a whole number is sincere.

Quantity or quality should never be divided or reduced.

Never zero, never negative;

The weight and size of the object will always increase.

The infinite total of two intersecting human sets is the sum of sincere love;

The love you feel for someone multiplies by itself and grows over time.

SITTING ON A CHAIR WITH TEDDY BEAR

You claim to have sat on a chair

Your favorite Teddy Bear Tucked under your hair

You relaxed on your chair?

You can tell by the glow of the fire that you are hugging, soothing and gently stroking a warmed Teddy bear.

You can tell that you have breathed in holiday air while being held by your loved ones.

The bear is a designated animal.

You remember a Christmas night filled with lights on the tree and an adorable little dog.

Your care is romantically embraced by the bear; I can see you sitting on a chair.

You have described a memorable night to me, with this special bear.

You and me on a night out.

TRUE LOVE LASTS

Like fine silver or gold, true love will not rust.

The original brilliance can be restored by polishing the tarnish.

A greater luster;

The true love does not seek fault or excuse for escape.

True love is eternal; it endures through all time

Love is eternal, regardless of the circumstances.

A GIFT TO YOU

I'm giving you a gift

You deserve praise for the work you have done and not what I would expect from you.

I'm giving you a gift,

What you are.

You are not what I would like you to be.

I'm giving you a gift,

We should not be rewarded for the things we do, but rather what we share.

I WON'T PROMISE

No, I won't promise you that

Tomorrow I'll love you

You will not be able to promise me that I'll love you tonight.

I can love you tomorrow

You can only love me now; or that I could love you tomorrow.

Now I am confident that it will last forever.

I LOVE YOU

Is it possible to say "I love You" if we really mean and feel it.

Is it possible to say "I Love You" without hedging or stammering?

Is it possible to say "I love You" without fear of regret?

How do we pronounce "I love you"?

How often and how clearly can we use these words?

How loudly can you say something?

Speak them out loudly and often.

POEMS ON LOVE
OF FAMILY,
CHILDREN,
FRIENDS, AND
NATURE

LOVE YOUR CHAIN

You will love the chain links!

A broken chain serves no purpose. Love your parents and love your kids.

You can love your siblings, your grandchildren and your grandparents.

They are important Links in a chain.

Above all else, you should love yourself.

All links of your chain are loved

A broken chain is useless.

THANK YOU MOTHER

You can't say anything.

You can't do anything else but thank her.

It is not enough to say thank you to your mother.

The mother, as a sacred temple for life is the trustee of God's seed.

The mother's touch is unique.

Her comforting voice is never replicated.

The greatest gift a mother can give is life. Her most important status is motherhood.

What a mom is, what she does or what other roles she may play are irrelevant.

A mother is always a mother. Thank you Mom, I love You.

MY CHILD, I'M GIVING YOU ADVICE

You should be true to yourself, your thoughts, feelings, eyes and ears.
Listen to the heart, but also to what your mind has to say.

Judgment;

Your Words will surely follow your kindness and wisdom.

Do not be afraid to take risks, but do exercise caution when you are tempted by emotions, confusion and false friendship;

Do not be jealous of other people's achievements or possessions.

Use or appreciate;

Eat less than you need to satisfy your appetite or drink more than is necessary for your thirst;

Do not offend those who oppose you, but listen to the spirits which favor you.

Develop as many of the common potentialities that you can and desire.

Do everything you can to live comfortably in your own conscience.

Be at peace within your own soul.

Always be courageous, but always remember Death's lure and lurking.

Respect the sacredness and dignity of all life by taking time to rest when tired or thinking when uncertain.

The natural order of the Universe

You should only follow your judgment and God's will.

Respect yourself, your family and yourself. Be the best you can be by improving yourself.

Live a meaningful and quality life. Do everything you can to help others who deserve it.

NOSTALGIA II

The difference between the two is that he was large and I small.

Both men are in sight;

Day and night, we worked and played with each other.

His memory will remain with me forever.

We shared our time together, sharing kindness and love.

You can find mule-driven carts for: Walking through a cornfield, feeding chickens, pigs, and hogs.

He was a man of many talents. I saw him drive, work two jobs, harvest and plant, make old-fashioned wines, care for his wife, and raise eight children.

As a seven-year old child, I was at his side as he died so bravely and peacefully in a tiny bed next to a window that had been opened.

Granddad, I will always miss you; Granddad, I will always love you.

LOVE IS...

The letter "L" stands for lament endured and laughter shared;

The letter "O" stands for obeying another.

Overindulgence in Time, okays, oughts, offering of oneself;

The vibrations of "V" represent the sacrifice value

Verification of emotions and vivid experiences are both common.

The letter "E" stands for Energy, eagerness and excitement.

Love is...

Love "Others" with

With "V"erve and vitality; "E"nthusiasm and expressiveness.

LOVE has no conditions, expectations, or Anticipation.

Love is...

A FRIEND

The friend you are looking for is

You are Special

Not against you, but being a good friend.

The state of one's mind is the state of their actions.

The special person who acts and thinks for the happiness of others.

To be a good friend, you must give of yourself.

Joy;

Being a good friend means receiving something from someone else.

To be a good friend, you must want to be one.

POEM BY A POET TO A FRIEND'S FRIEND

I am asked to compose a short poem for a distant friend;

Even though you are miles apart, someone that you know well and have been friends with for years.

It is a request that I find unusual, but one you will not deny because it appears You care.

It is worth the time spent to think of such valuable thoughts for a lasting bond

Each part is sought

You've been talking on the phone for years, but you are rarely as close.

It seems that Two people have discovered the true essence of friendship.

A mutual concern and a lot of shared experience;

This poet ends with a good thought of my work.

Your friendship will last forever.

LET US LOVE CHILD

We love you child

Life is precious, and it should be treated as such.

Children are not to be viewed as objects of frustration or sensuality, but as something we should love.

Our future is their future.

We can love our children better by stopping their suffering.

We must wipe the images of horror from their minds.

Keep harsh words out of their ears; Block unnatural trauma and pain from their little hearts, as we teach them how to live naturally.

Healthy living, realistic life style

We love you child

We have loved, so let us love the child

We should love our child as we would have loved ourselves

We should love ourselves.

I LOVE YOU

You're in love with me, you're in love with me, or I am in love

My son.

What a sweet gift from God! How joyous, how refreshing, and what a delight.

The light of God is shining on you, my son

You've got me in love

Hold him.

It is to kiss the little lips of his father,

It is to experience the gift of Your creation.

Ah, the light that shines in my day and night!

My son, my love.

I NEVER SAW

I have never seen a woman do that.

She loved her son so much. I have never seen a woman who was as passionate about a child.

The parents of this baby boy were so happy with their son; I have never seen such a loving parent.

They loved their son, but I had never seen them until I met ourselves.

THE SENSES OF MY LOVE

The things I see and hear I love; the things I touch I love; what I smell I also loves.

The beauty of trees, rivers, mountains, seas, music, food, birds and people.

Beauty is something I've always loved.

Particularly when I've paid

I am able to feel their environment.

A FLOWER

The flower-

The beauty of its temporality, the fragility of its petals and its variegated colors.

The colors of the rainbow are red, yellow, orange, pink, violet, and white.

The flower-

What a simple and sweet smell! A beautiful thing in full bloom.

The thing we do to express our Love, thought, and care.

The flower-

Wearing one's own hair is to touch.

Holidays and other special occasions are everywhere.

The flower is a beautiful example of this.

It is a blessing to our surroundings and brings joy.

The sick, the bereaved and the well.

The flower is a beautiful example of this.

The flower is to be loved, and to see it, smell it, or hold it.

We are here.

A FLOWER ODE

In the light of the sun And in the secret of the night's cover, Oh Flower! Show off your beauty.

The dew of dawn and April's tears will show you your beauty.

Flower, source of the florist's dream to make your gift.

A flower?

It is a miracle that God has repeated His grace through the green arms of trees and plants, with their outstretched branches.

Smile for me, Oh Flower; smile so that I may see your love.

TREES OF MAINE

They stand tall and straight in Maine, USA.

Pine, Fir, and Spruce

Through branches so broad and ordered in symmetry they bid welcome and goodbye.

It is a character that's both robust and calm.

The carpeting of vast acreages in mosaics is made up by trees.

Greens in various shades;

More trees!

The sun, the clouds and calm skies are all God's creations.

Thank you for your presence and message, Trees of Maine.

The Trees of Maine wish you happy and long stays.

Printed in Great Britain
by Amazon